Two Mrs. Gibsons

STORY BY TOYOMI IGUS   PICTURES BY DARYL WELLS

CHILDREN'S BOOK PRESS

SAN FRANCISCO, CALIFORNIA

I once knew two Mrs. Gibsons.

This Mrs. Gibson was tall. Her skin was the color of chocolate. She was born in America in a place called Tennessee.

This Mrs. Gibson was
small. Her skin was the
color of vanilla. She was
born in Japan in a place
called Gifu.

This Mrs. Gibson gave hugs that were like being wrapped up in a great big fat bearskin rug. "Come here and give me some sugar!" she would say.

This Mrs. Gibson gave hugs that were like being wrapped up in a light, down-filled comforter. At bedtime she'd stroke my hair and hum "Sakura" until I fell asleep.

This Mrs. Gibson was loud.

She had a big laugh, and a big voice, which would get louder when she was angry or when she was singing. And she seemed to be singing all the time.

"This little light of mine I'm gonna let it shine!"

This Mrs. Gibson was quiet.

She would cover her mouth when she laughed, so you could never see her teeth. And when she was angry, she'd get even quieter.

This Mrs. Gibson had small hands that could make the littlest, prettiest strokes of a pen when she would write our names in Japanese.

Ku-mi-ki.
A-ki-mi.
To-yo-mi.
Yo-shi-te-ru.

This Mrs. Gibson had big hands. They looked like they covered all the keys on the piano when she played her favorite spirituals.

"This little light of mine, I'm gonna let it shine!
Let it shine!
Let it shine!
Let it shine!"

Sometimes this Mrs. Gibson would look kind of sad and then she would let me dress up in one of the kimonos she had packed away in an old trunk. "These very special," she would say as she tied the *obi* around my waist. "Don't get dirty."

The other Mrs. Gibson's clothes were much too big for me to dress up in, but I liked to wear her fancy hats. "This is my Sunday-go-to-meetin' hat," she would say as she'd take the long pointy hat pin out of my hand. "Don't get it dirty, now."

In the evening in the garden, this Mrs. Gibson would help me make magical lamps by catching fireflies and putting them in a jelly jar. They would glow and glow — and then we'd let them go.

Later at dinner time, this Mrs. Gibson
would make more magic. Her hands would
turn little bits of napkins into a whole flock
of long-necked cranes. We would throw
them into the air where they would fly high
and then flutter down to the ground.
"Happy birds," she would always say.

This Mrs. Gibson always had a pot of rice cooking. We would eat it with bits of meat and vegetables on it, with plenty of *shoyu*. Any time we were hungry, she could take her long chopsticks and stir up dinner in the blink of an eye.

This Mrs. Gibson always had a pot of greens cooking. Turnip greens, dandelion greens, mustard greens from the garden. Everything she cooked seemed to take a long, long time.

This Mrs. Gibson had short curly hair that she would oil and braid up every night while she listened to the radio. She liked to braid my hair too, but she would always give me one big fat braid that would hang down over my forehead.

I didn't like that braid, so I would go to the other Mrs. Gibson, and she'd take it out. This Mrs. Gibson used to have long stick-straight hair, but she cut it short and tried to make it curly. She said she wanted to be more American.

This Mrs. Gibson's other name was Kazumi.
Everyone called her Kaz or Connie because they
couldn't pronounce Kazumi.

I called her Mommy because she was my mother.

This Mrs. Gibson's other name was Viola. Everyone called her Vi or Reverend Gibson, because she was a church minister.

I called her Nanny because she was my grandmother.

I once knew two Mrs. Gibsons.

They were very different, but they had a lot in common.

They both loved my Daddy and they both loved me.

When I was a little girl—long before I ever thought of becoming a writer—my family lived for a time at my grandmother's house in Cedar Rapids, Iowa. While my father went to law school, my mother, Kazumi Tamori Gibson, and my grandmother, Viola Alice Willis Gibson, took care of us. This is a story about that time and about the two most important women in my life—one who was Japanese and another who was African American. Whenever I start to think that the many problems people have with one another will never be resolved, I remember my two Mrs. Gibsons, who showed me that love can overcome all differences and transcend all boundaries.   —*Toyomi Igus*

Toyomi Igus is the Managing Editor for *CAAS Publications*, the press at UCLA's Center for African American Studies. She is the author and editor of several books for young people, including *Great Women in the Struggle*, profiles of African American women (Just Us Books). Toyomi lives in Los Angeles with her husband, Darrow, her two children, Kazumi and Kenji, and Easter, the dog.

Daryl Wells is a painter and a former art teacher for the Los Angeles Unified School District. She has worked with young people to create many public murals. A graduate of the Rhode Island School of Design, Daryl is currently pursuing her Master's Degree at the Slade School of Fine Art in London, England. She is a native of Los Angeles, California.

For Kazumi, Kenji, Jozen, Noel, Brandon, Christian, and Daylin who never got to meet the two Mrs. Gibsons. —T.I.
To my niece, Beatrice Xochitl Johnson: May your diverse heritage be a source of inspiration and pride for you always. —D.W.

Editors: Harriet Rohmer and David Schecter • Design: Katherine Tillotson • Editorial/Production Assistant: Laura Atkins
Publisher & Executive Director (current): Lorraine García-Nakata
Thanks to Yuri Okabayashi, Barbara Wells, Kenji and Kazumi Igus, Jean Gima, Corinne Griggs, Claire Wells, Allen Mikaelian, and Stephen Mason.
And thanks to the staff of Children's Book Press: Jenny Brandt, Andrea Durham, Janet Levin, Emily Romero and Stephanie Sloan.

Children's Book Press is a 501(c)(3) nonprofit organization (Fed Tax ID # 94-2298885). Our work is made possible in part by: AT&T Foundation, John Crew and Sheila Gadsden, San Francisco Foundation, San Francisco Arts Commission, Horizons Foundation, National Endowment for the Arts, Union Bank of California, Children's Book Press Board of Directors, Elizabeth Ports, and the Anonymous Fund of the Greater Houston Community Foundation. Original printing of this book was supported in part by the California Arts Council. To make a contribution or receive a catalog, visit our website: www.childrensbookpress.org

Library of Congress Cataloging-in-Publication Data
Igus, Toyomi.
Two Mrs. Gibsons / story by Toyomi Igus; pictures by Daryl Wells   p.   cm.
    Summary: The biracial daughter of an African American father and a Japanese mother fondly recalls growing up with her mother and her father's mother, two very different but equally loving women.
ISBN 978-0-89239-170-7 (paperback)
[1. Grandmother—Fiction. 2. Mothers—Fiction. 3. Interracial marriage—Fiction. 4. Japanese—United States—Fiction. 5. Afro-Americans—Fiction.] I. Wells, Daryl, ill. II. Title.
PZ7.126TW   1995
[E}—dc20   95-37572   CIP   AC

Distributed to the book trade by Publisher's Group West.
Printed in Hong Kong through Marwin Productions.
10   9   8   7